Eyebrows

By Robin Twiddy

KidHaven PUBLISHING

Published in 2023 by
KidHaven Publishing, an Imprint of Greenhaven Publishing, LLC
2544 Clinton St., Buffalo, NY 14224

© 2022 Booklife Publishing
This edition is published by arrangement with Booklife Publishing

Written by: Robin Twiddy
Edited by: William Anthony
Designed by: Danielle Rippengill
Image Credits: All images are courtesy of Shutterstock.com, unless otherwise specified. With thanks to Getty Images, Thinkstock Photo and iStockphoto. Front Cover - Talirina, s_maria, Idol Design. 2 -KenoKickit. 4&5 - Rawpixel.com, Anatoliy Karlyuk. 6&7 - EJ Nickerson, ROMAN DZIUBALO, ozrimoz. 8&9 - Katia Regina Silveira, Sabphoto. 10&11 - pathdoc, snob, wavebreakmedia. 12&13 - CebotariN, KenoKickit. 14&15 - Amelia Fox, Nejron Photo, Stuart Monk, eyepark, Phovoir. 16&17 - Matt Hahnewald, spaxiax. 18&19 - Nora Yusuf, Debra Anderson, Belozerova Daria. 20&21 - SeventyFour, MARUIZ, Krakenimages.com. 22&23 - Sudowoodo. 24 - KenoKickit.

Cataloging-in-Publication Data

Names: Twiddy, Robin.
Title: Eyebrows / Robin Twiddy.
Description: New York : KidHaven Publishing, 2023. | Series: Brilliant bodies
Identifiers: ISBN 9781534542822 (pbk.) | ISBN 9781534542846 (library bound) | ISBN 9781534542853 (ebook)
Subjects: LCSH: Face--Juvenile literature. | Human physiology--Juvenile literature. | Human body--Juvenile literature.
Classification: LCC QM535.T835 2023 | DDC 611'.92--dc23

All rights reserved.
No part of this book may be reproduced in any form without permission in writing from the publisher, except by a reviewer.

Manufactured in the United States of America

CPSIA compliance information: Batch #CWKH23: For further information contact Greenhaven Publishing LLC at 1-844-317-7404.

Please visit our website, www.greenhavenpublishing.com.
For a free color catalog of all our high-quality books, call toll free 1-844-317-7404 or fax 1-844-317-7405.

Find us on

Contents

Page 4	Bodies Are Brilliant
Page 6	What Are Eyebrows?
Page 8	What Do They Do?
Page 10	Making Faces
Page 12	Talking with Our Eyebrows
Page 14	Different Eyebrows
Page 16	Old Eyebrows
Page 18	Not Eyebrows
Page 20	Brilliant Without
Page 22	Brilliant Bits of Bodies
Page 24	Match the Eyebrows

Bodies Are Brilliant

Brilliant bodies are everywhere. You have one and so do all your friends.

Our brilliant bodies have lots of brilliant parts. One of these brilliant parts is our eyebrows.

What Are Eyebrows?

Eyebrows are the hairs that grow together just above our eyes.

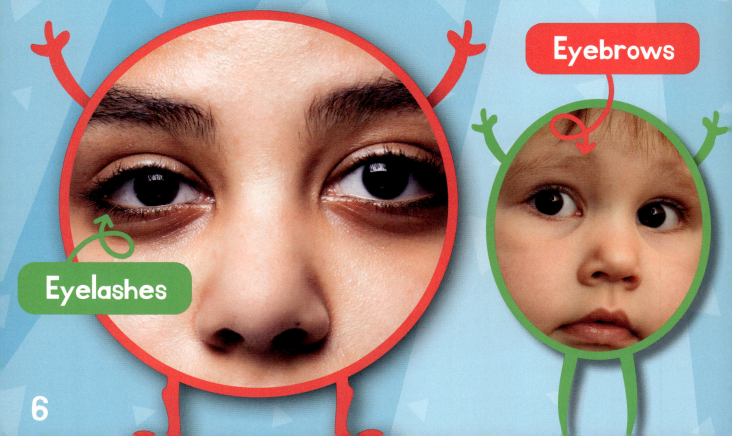

Eyelashes

Eyebrows

What Do They Do?

Eyebrows help stop things such as rain and sweat from getting into our eyes.

Eyebrows also help keep sunlight out of our eyes.

Making Faces

One of the other brilliant things that eyebrows do is help us show how we are feeling.

The shape of our eyebrows can show if we are happy, sad, angry, and more.

Talking with Our Eyebrows

We can make lots of fun faces with our eyebrows.

Different Eyebrows

Eyebrows come in different colors, just like the hair on our heads.

Whatever shape your eyebrows are, they are brilliant!

Eyebrows can be different shapes. Some people have thick eyebrows and others have thinner ones.

Old Eyebrows

When men get older, their eyebrows might grow even faster than they did before.

Some men might go bald when they get older, but their eyebrows will keep growing.

Not Eyebrows

Lots of animals look like they have eyebrows just like us.

Cats' whiskers help them feel what is around them.

Cats have special whiskers above their eyes. These look like long eyebrows.

Brilliant Without

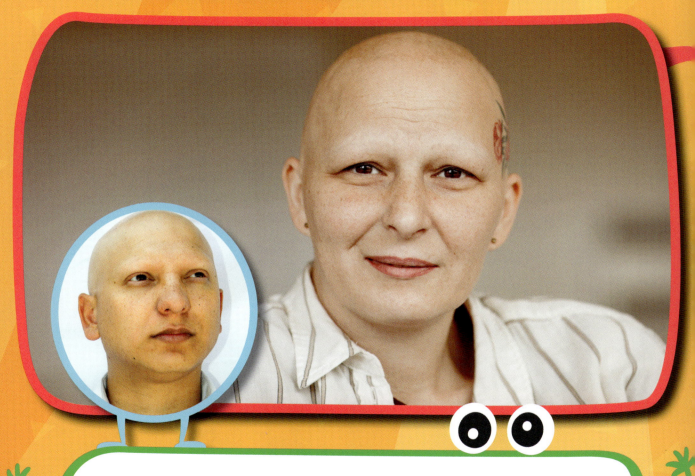

Some people don't have eyebrows. Their bodies don't grow hair like other people's.

These bodies are brilliant, just like any others. All bodies are brilliant.

Brilliant Bits of Bodies

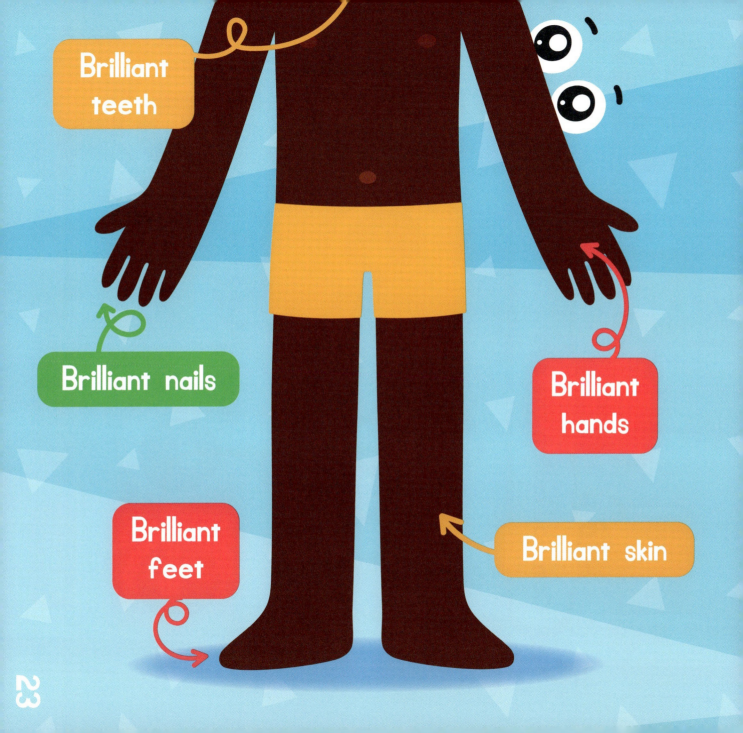

Match the Eyebrows

Can you match the eyebrows to the feelings?

Happy   Scared   Sad   Angry